Daryl Cagle's "BARACK OBAMA" Coloring Book!

Artwork and text by Daryl Cagle

Copyright Daryl Cagle. All Rights Reserved.
Follow Daryl Cagle on Twitter: @dcagle
Read Daryl's blog at: DarylCagle.com
See all of our great cartoons at: Cagle.com
Visit PoliticalCartoons.com to reprint any of Daryl's cartoons.
Published by: Cagle Cartoons, Inc., visit CagleWorld.com to learn more about us.
For sales contact: editor@cagle.com or call (805) 969-2829.

Published by Cagle Cartoons, Inc.
ISBN-13: 978-0692710593
ISBN-10: 0692710590
Printed in the United States of America, First Printing: May, 2016

Obama Transforms

They started out looking different, but with his cozy support of Wall Street and his eagerness to jump into foreign conflicts, Obama grew to look more like George W. Bush.

DARYL
CAGLE

POLITICALCARTOONS.COM

Capitol Hill Stumbles

The Republican Congress tripped up Obama at every turn.

DARYL CAGLE
POLITICALCARTOONS.COM

Nails in Hillary's Coffin

In the 2008 primaries, Obama took a long time putting Hillary away.

DARYL CAGLE

John McCain and the Crashing Economy

The economy crashed at just the right time for Obama's 2008 campaign.

Sure to Win in 2008

Everything lined up for an Obama victory in 2008.

DARYL CAGLE

Fighting off Romney in 2012

It wasn't too hard holding off Romney's challenge in 2012.

DARYL CAGLE

Fox News Denies Reality

Fox News portrayed Romney as a sure winner in 2012 - up until the bitter end.

Wrapping Themselves in the Flag
Both Obama and Romney claimed to be more of a patriot in 2012.

Israel's President Disses Obama

The Republicans invited Israeli President and Obama critic, Benjamin Netanyahu, to speak to a joint session of Congress, snubbing Obama.

DARYL CAGLE

Natanyahu and Obama Don't Get Along

It was pretty clear that these guys didn't like each other.

Tongue Tied with Iran

Nuclear negotiations with Iran didn't seem to be going well, seen here with Iran's Supreme Leader, Ali Khamenei.

DARYL
CAGLE

USA   IRAN

PoliticalCartoons.com

The Iran Nuclear Deal

To the consternation of Republicans, Obama made a deal with Iran with the support of Iran's moderate president Hassan Rouhani.

DARYL
CAGLE
POLITICALCARTOONS.COM

Another Iran Handshake

Obama and Iran's Supreme Leader seemed to have different motivations.

Kissing the Saudi King's Butt

Obama was widely criticized by conservatives for bowing to the king of Saudi Arabia. He opposed efforts in congress to allow 9/11 victims to sue the Saudi government during a later visit with the king.

NO WORRIES. WE WON'T LET 9-11 VICTIMS SUE YOU.

BOWING TO THE SAUDI KING, PART TWO.

Putin Defends Assad in Syria

Russian President Putin's top priority in Syria seemed to be attacking the "moderate" rebels that Obama supported.

YOU'VE GOT IT ALL WRONG. I DON'T HAVE MY DOG ON A LEASH — I'M ON **HIS** LEASH. AND THAT'S NOT **YOUR** DOG HE JUST ATE.

MODERATE REBELS

OBama GETS IT ALL WRONG.

Jumping Back Into Iraq

Iraq predictably fell apart when American troops withdrew, and Obama jumped back in.

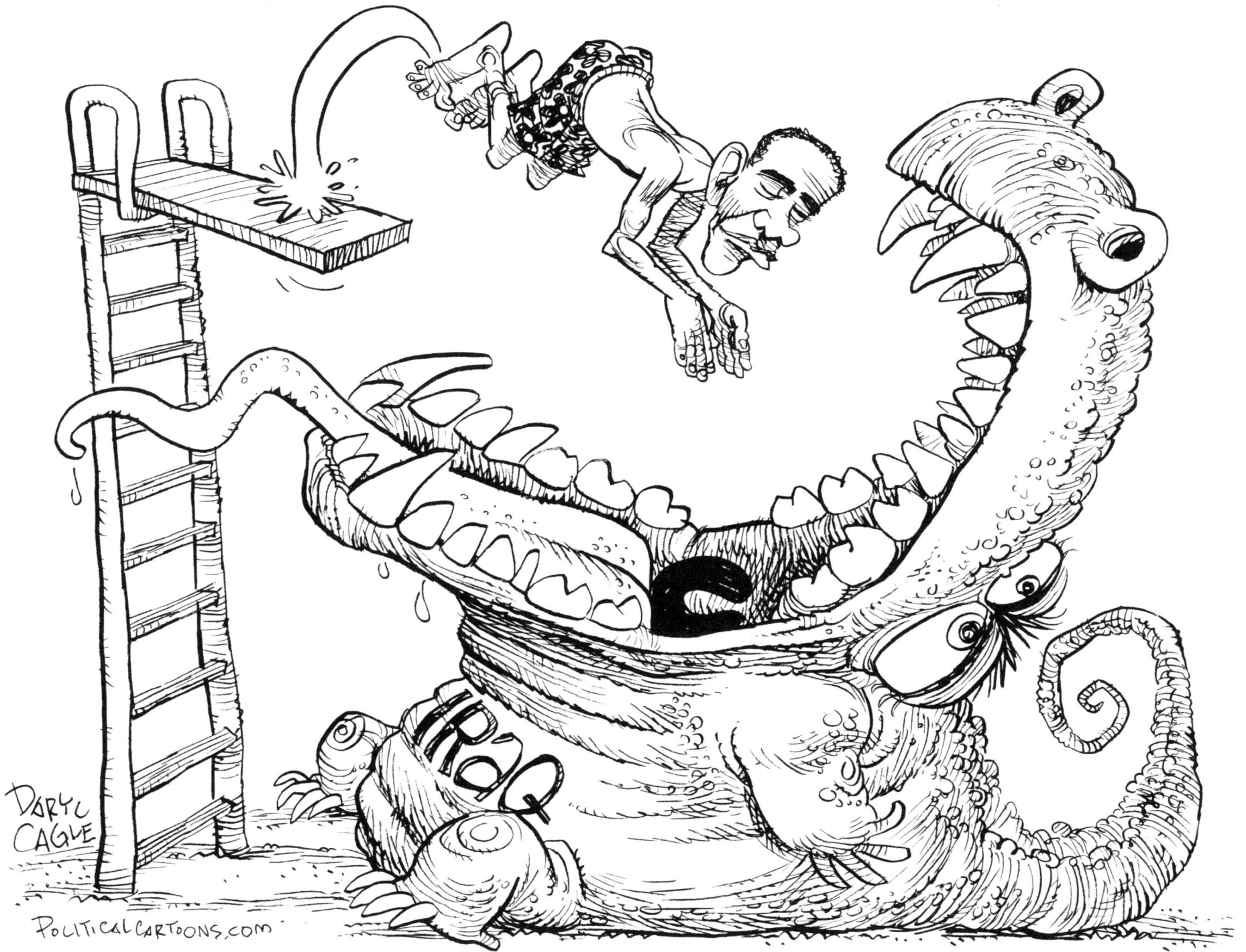

DARYL CAGLE

POLITICALCARTOONS.COM

IRaq

Pouring More Troops Into Afghanistan

After pulling back from Afghanistan, Obama began sending troops back.

MORE TROOPS TO STAY

Afghanistan

DARYL CAGLE

POLITICALCARTOONS.COM

Shocking Mess in the Middle East

Obama meddled in the Middle East as the Arab Spring revolts combined to make a highly-charged mess.

ARAB SPRING

IRAQ AFGHANISTAN PAKISTAN

EGYPT

SYRIA

IRAN

POLITICALCARTOONS.COM

DARYL CAGLE

Revolution in Egypt

Obama continued to pour money into Egypt as their democratically elected, "Muslim Brotherhood" strongman president Morsi was overthrown..

DARYL CAGLE POLITICALCARTOONS.COM

Not a Coup

Egypt's president fell victim to the Arab Spring and was overthrown in a military coup, but Obama didn't acknowledge that because, under the law, he would have to stop giving billions of dollars to Egypt if there was a military coup there.

Republicans Can't Stand Obama's Vocabulary

Nothing bothers Republicans more than Obama's refusal to say the words "Islamic Terrorists".

Osama Bin Laden is Killed

Obama approved a risky raid to kill the mastermind behind the 9/11 attacks.

DARYL CAGLE

Pakistan is Annoyed

The raid to kill Osama Bin Laden didn't sit well with Pakistan.

More Money for Pakistan

Obama continued giving billions of dollars to Pakistan.

Spineless Obama

Even though Obama was constantly meddling in the Middle East, Republicans accused him of being spineless, and not doing enough.

Love Those Drones

Obama led a massive expansion in the use of unmanned drones to kill "enemy combatants" in the Middle East.

DARYL CAGLE
CAGLECARTOONS.COM

Drones are Unpopular

Civilian casualties in drone attacks hurt America's image around the world.

TOMAHAWK

Daryl Cagle PoliticalCartoons.com

Ukraine and ISIS

Continuing crises made life uncomfortable for Obama.

ISIS or ISIL

UKRAINE

RUSSIA

DARYL CAGLE POLITICALCARTOONS.COM

North Korea
Kim Jong Un was unpleasant for both America and China.

YAP YAP
YAP YAP YAP
YAP ARF YIP YAP
YAP YAP

CHINA

DARYL CAGLE POLITICALCARTOONS.COM

Obama Grows in Office

As the years ticked by, Obama grew more and more unpopular.

JANUARY 2009

JULY 2009

DECEMBER 2009

MARCH 2010

JULY 2010

DARYL CAGLE

Charlie Hebdo Killings in Paris

Obama, along with much of America, showed little sympathy for the victims of the terror attack.

Spying on Everyone
Edward Snowden revealed the vast spy network and surveillance on all Americans and our allies overseas.

Brushing Off the GOP

Obama dealt with annoying Republicans.

DARYL CAGLE
POLITICALCARTOONS.COM

CAGLE.COM

Leaders in Congress
Obama didn't take any bull.

Obamacare

Republicans did all they could to stop Obama's healthcare plan, and they failed.

DARYL CAGLE

Crazy, Never Ending Opposition to Obamacare
Obama's healthcare legislation continued to drive Republicans crazy.

Santa Obama

Republicans see Obama giving away the store.

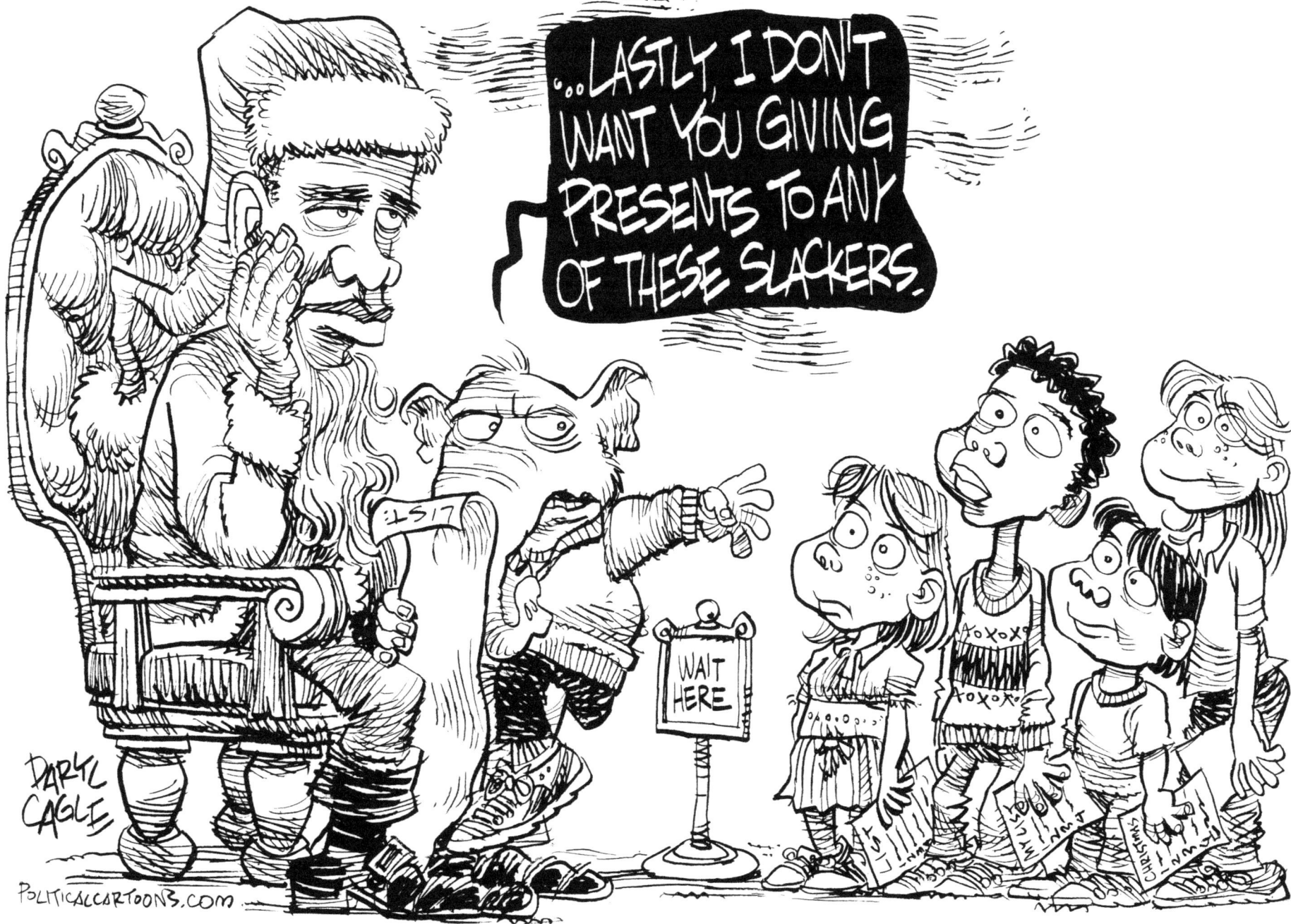

A Pen and a Phone

Obama famously said he has a "pen and a phone" when it became clear that he couldn't get his agenda through congress. Obama signed executive orders to get around congress.

DARYL CAGLE
POLITICALCARTOONS.COM

Forward

Obama's 2012 slogan "Forward" seemed ironic.

Anchor

Obama's sinking popularity seemed sure to sink the Democrats in 2016 – until Donald Trump came along.

DARYL CAGLE
POLITICALCARTOONS.com

For the past 35 years, Daryl Cagle has been one of America's most prolific cartoonists. He worked for 15 years with Jim Henson's Muppets, illustrating scores of books, magazines, calendars, and all manner of products. Daryl still sees pigs, frogs, Sesame Street and Fraggle Rock characters when he closes his eyes. He worked as the editorial cartoonist in Hawaii, then was the cartoonist for the Washington Post's Slate.com site and msnbc.com. Daryl is America's most widely syndicated editorial cartoonist.

To see more of Daryl's work visit DarylCagle.com. To reprint cartoons from Daryl and from the top editorial cartoonists around the world, visit PoliticalCartoons.com or call (805) 969-2829.

Collect All of the Daryl Cagle Coloring Books at CagleBook.com